8 Fundamentals to Earn a Million
Dollars
in Network Marketing

Bonus Report:
The Top *10* Million Dollar
Recruiting Tips to
Explode Your MLM Business NOW!

John Di Lemme

8 Fundamentals to Earn a Million Dollars in Network Marketing Plus Bonus Report: The Top 10 Recruiting Tips to Explode Your MLM Business Now! © 2008 John Di Lemme

Di Lemme Development Group, Inc.
931 Village Boulevard
Suite 905-366
West Palm Beach, Florida 33409-1939
(561) 847-3467
www.ConservativeBusinessJournal.com

This book is designed to provide competent and reliable information regarding the subject matters covered. However, it is sold with the understanding that the author is not engaged in rendering legal, financial, or other professional advice. Laws and practices often vary from state to state and if legal or other expert assistance is required, the services of a professional should be sought. The author specifically disclaims any liability that is incurred from the use and/or application of the contents of this book.

ISBN: 978-0-557-01251-0

Password Tracker

Website	User Name	Password

Password Tracker

Website	User Name	Password

Password Tracker

Website	User Name	Password

Password Tracker

Website	User Name	Password

Password Tracker

Website	User Name	Password

Password Tracker

Website	User Name	Password

Password Tracker

Website	User Name	Password

Password Tracker

Website	User Name	Password

Password Tracker

Website	User Name	Password

Password Tracker

Website	User Name	Password

Password Tracker

Website	User Name	Password

Password Tracker

Website	User Name	Password

Password Tracker

Website	User Name	Password

Password Tracker

Website	User Name	Password

Password Tracker

Website	User Name	Password

Password Tracker

Website	User Name	Password

Password Tracker

Website	User Name	Password

Password Tracker

Website	User Name	Password

Password Tracker

Website	User Name	Password

Password Tracker

Website	User Name	Password

Password Tracker

Website	User Name	Password

Password Tracker

Website	User Name	Password

Password Tracker

Website	User Name	Password

Password Tracker

Website	User Name	Password

Password Tracker

Website	User Name	Password

Password Tracker

Website	User Name	Password

Password Tracker

Website	User Name	Password

Password Tracker

Website	User Name	Password

Password Tracker

Website	User Name	Password

Password Tracker

Website	User Name	Password

Password Tracker

Website	User Name	Password

Password Tracker

Website	User Name	Password

Password Tracker

Website	User Name	Password

Password Tracker

Website	User Name	Password

Password Tracker

Website	User Name	Password

Password Tracker

Website	User Name	Password

Password Tracker

Website	User Name	Password

Password Tracker

Website	User Name	Password

About the Author

John Di Lemme launched his writing and speaking career over 20 years ago after achieving 7 figure success in the industry of network marketing.

Since that time, John has gone on to achieve monumental success as a speaker, author, capitalism strategist, conservative political commentator, podcaster, and founder of the Conservative Business Journal.

As you read this book, remember that it was written by someone who achieved real results in Network Marketing and understands what it takes to achieve record-breaking success.

Fundamental #1: Being Successful is a Choice that YOU Make.

We all need to realize that the power to choose is one of the greatest gifts that we possess, and we must fully utilize this power in every situation. God gives us the power to choose – let's make sure we treat the gift with respect and use it to achieve our ultimate goals in life!

"Each failure is a stepping stone to Success, which in turn will become a very long and lovely stone walkway into the castle of your DREAMS!" – John Di Lemme

Being successful is a choice that YOU make! Your success isn't a matter of luck; it's simply a matter of choices that you make. Success isn't something you can wait for. Instead, it's something you'll achieve with effort. Things won't turn up in this world until you turn them up.

One's philosophy is not best expressed in words; it is expressed in the choices one makes. In the long run, we shape our lives and we shape ourselves. The process never ends until we die. And, the choices we make are ultimately our own responsibility. - Eleanor Roosevelt

You can choose to be lazy (not prospect) or ambitious (prospect like crazy). Stop and think about your choice again. You always make your own choices!

The greatest opportunity in your life is where you are right now, not where you will be tomorrow. Do what you have to do NOW to make things happen and reveal the future that you've only dreamed about.

Massive Success is right in front of you and within your reach, but will you choose it?

Fundamental #2: Find Your Why and Fly.

You must know your WHY in order to deal with issues such as:

• Why recruit?
• Why deal with rejection as you build your dream?
• Why show up early and work late into the night?
• Why deal with certain clients?
• Why introduce your business consistently to people daily regardless of their response?
• Why work and plan over the weekend?

"You must be absolutely clear about your goal and be relentless in the pursuit of your WHY." – John Di Lemme

Reading your WHY card for the first seven minutes upon rising is the secret to cementing your WHY into your spirit. This simple yet powerful morning habit will direct your actions as you progress through your day. You will begin to see yourself handling your challenges a little differently.

You'll be excited and know that all of this is worth it, because you know your WHY. You will deal with those challenges and forge

3

forward, never looking back. An example of a WHY card is:

"I am dealing with all the challenges of building my MLM business today, because my WHY is to spend more time with my family, provide for my children's education, and have the finances needed to take regular family vacations and be a mentor to my kids. I am donating and tithing a percentage of my earnings to my church or favorite organization. I am making a difference today as a Profit- Producing, Fear-Demolishing, Record- Breaking, Action-Taking, Eye-Opening, Mind-Blowing, Fired-Up and Laser-Focused MLM Millionaire Champion."

I challenge you to re-evaluate where you are today, where you want to be five years from now and decide to take action! Write a personal WHY card and begin reading it daily. To discover more about the power of a Why Card and the "10 Life Lessons on How to Find Your Why NOW and Achieve Ultimate Success", visit
www.ConservativeMarketplace.com.

Fundamental #3: Say YES to Rejection!

Rejection is the #1 reason for ninety-nine percent of all failures in life. You must realize that as you plan to achieve uncommon results in life for you and your family you will face rejection.

Remember, it is easier for someone to reject you, point a finger at you and say things like "you will never succeed, you are crazy and stop dreaming", rather than them taking action to change their own lives! As they point one finger at you, remember there are three fingers pointing right back at them.

We have the power to choose to fulfill our dreams, and choosing to accept rejection by dealing with it is the key to the fulfillment of your dream! While you pay the price to reach that dream, your #1 enemy will be rejection. You must expect it, love the challenge and know that you are heading in the right direction.

A major step in paying the price is hitting massive rejection. In that instance, you must decide whether to get fired up or fall down to the enemy! Rejection is emotional. The average person will wear their emotions on their sleeve for most of their life unless they decide to put those emotions aside and use that rejection as a driving force to reach their ultimate goal in life!

You live for your "WHY" – your ultimate dream! You must live by faith and know that rejection is your enemy.   You have a victorious spirit to conquer that enemy! Rejection can try to deter you, but those qualities that you possess will ultimately make you successful in achieving your WHY! As you say YES to rejection, you are beginning to win in the game called life.

To me it was like yesterday, I was a 24 year old stuttering kid living in New York, stuck in a rut with no dreams or goals and no money in the bank! What does that mean to you? It means if you are presently in a state of rejection, you must forge forward and, most importantly, upwards towards the fulfillment of your WHY!!

I am always very enthused to address the topic of REJECTION!   How you handle rejection is in direct proportion to how you maintain a persistent level of action in order to feel fulfilled and find your WHY in life.   As a super-achiever in life (which means you have your WHY in place), you are driven to fulfill your personal goals set for you on a daily basis. In the course of this daily action, you will inevitably encounter rejection and the incredible power it exerts over you!

Just when you are feeling great and your business is beginning to grow, you will experience rejection. Out of nowhere, it will slap you right in the face like an icy, cold wind and your little voice inside begins to doubt whether or not you can really achieve what you initially set out for.
YOU MUST LEARN TO LOVE REJECTION! You must become excited when you get rejected while at the same time you continue to forge ahead no matter how much that rejection hurts!

The most successful people are those who have felt the pains of rejection, but because of their DETERMINATION they pressed onward and won the game. As you are building your business, you need to set a goal and continue toward it regardless of the degree of discomfort that rejection may be causing you! Rejection is an extremely negative force; therefore, it is to your benefit to channel this force to produce positive results!

Thomas Edison is famous for the 10,000 ways that a person couldn't create a light bulb due to his numerous attempts to reach his goal - creating a light bulb! As we all know, he eventually succeeded. Rather than seeing his previous attempts as a negative force, he utilized all that he had learned through the many failures to produce the positive result of achieving his goal!

You too will develop incredible character as you continue to build your business, regardless of the rejection that you experience along the way. As a super-achiever, you will use your knowledge of rejection and its power to your advantage. Expect rejection, love rejection, learn from rejection and you will succeed!

Fundamental #4: Failure Means that You Are Almost There.

We all know as we progress towards the achievement of our MLM goals and dreams that we will fail repeatedly, and then all of a sudden we will achieve our ultimate outcome! You must truly internalize the need to fail in life.

Most people fail more between the ages of 16-25 and then they don't fail ever again in life, which means they never SUCCEED! At the age 25, the majority of people lose their steam and decide to live a "normal" life instead of designing a lifestyle for themselves and their families. I can tell you with conviction that I have failed numerous times in my life.

My parents used to say..."but John you went to college just go get a JOB!" As entrepreneurs, we all know that we never just go get any job, because whatever we do has our life-print on it, which represents our potential.

Here are a couple of famous people that failed before they finally succeeded:

A relatively unsuccessful marketer of restaurant equipment, he didn't sell his first hamburger until age 52. At a time when many people prepare for retirement, Ray Kroc built McDonald's from a handful of hamburger stands into the world's largest food chain.

Walt Disney was fired by a newspaper for lacking ideas. He also went bankrupt several times before he built Disneyland.

The question that I have for you now is "Do you realize how excited you must be about your failures, because those failures ultimately become your successes?" As many of my students have heard me say, "Experience is what you receive when you do not achieve what you desire."

I suggest that you put this material on your desk where you can read it every day to remind yourself about Ray Kroc and Walt Disney and say to yourself, "What is MY story going to be?" You need to fail in order to ultimately succeed in LIFE. In success language, failure means that you're almost there. So, don't give up!

Fundamental #5: Habits – Your Greatest MLM Helper or Your Heaviest MLM Burden?

H-A-B-I-T...When 97% of people hear this word, a negative thought pops up in their minds. Typically, most people think of a habit as being negative, because that's what they've always been taught.

The secret to your future lies in your daily habits so ask yourself right now, *"Are my habits today going to help me achieve my WHY in life?"* This is a life-empowering question so be honest with yourself in determining your answer. I feel the following excerpt is definitely the best explanation of a habit:

"I am your constant companion. I am your greatest helper or your heaviest burden. I will push you onward or drag you down to failure. I am completely at your command. Half the things you do, you might just as well turn over to me, and I will be able to do them quickly and correctly. I am easily managed; you must merely be firm with me. Show me exactly how you want something done, and after a few lessons I will do it automatically. I am the servant of all great men. And, alas, of all failures as well. Those who are great, I have made great. Those who are failures, I have made failures. I am not a machine, though I work with all the precision of a machine. Plus, the intelligence of a man. You may run me for profit, or run me for ruin; it makes no difference to me. Take me, train me, be firm with me and I will put the world at your feet. Be easy with me, and I will destroy you. Who am I? I am a HABIT!" – Author Unknown

One of my daily habits, which is also the foundation of my life, is investing 60 to 90 minutes each and every morning feeding my body physically by exercising and feeding my mental spirit by reading and/or listening to a inspirational motivational messages.

This habit warms me up for the day ahead. Everyone washes their physical body and feeds their body every morning, but 97% of people will find an excuse about why they cannot find the "TIME" to invest in a habit of feeding their MINDS!

This parallels the statistic that 97% of people are dead or dead broke by the age 65. I consider this particular daily habit of mine to be the driving force behind my ability to consistently maintain my intense focus on the journey of success and living a dream life.

Is it easy all the time? Of course not, but when it becomes a habit – you will do it! If you commit today to begin each morning warming yourself up for the day ahead by feeding your mental spirit, your entire life will change in a positive fashion very quickly.

It's like driving a race car with the emergency brake on and you try to speed ahead, but you can't move. You stay in the same location with your wheels spinning, burning up, making a lot of noise, but not going anywhere!

All it takes is to release the brake and you will fly towards your WHY in life! You need to review your current habits and ask yourself, *"Would I recommend MY habits to someone I truly love and care about?"* Your entire MLM future lies in your daily habits —positive or negative.

You have the most powerful force right now in your hands, the ability to decide to commit to habits that will empower you to achieve your Why and build your MLM dreams.

Fundamental #6: The Power of Storytelling

Each and every day as we are building our businesses, we all know the key to a successful MLM presentation is marketing our product to the end-line consumer and/or sponsoring a new teammate.

In the sales process, you are fighting many different types of animals. For most of us who are in direct sales, you have 45 minutes to present a product/business concept and make a person believe in you, your product and, more importantly, ask them to make a decision that they want what you are offering.

I often speak about one of the most powerful key business strategies, the power of storytelling. When you are presenting your business, it is very easy for you to get very factual and completely lose the interest of your prospect.

When you tell a story about the success of someone who is using the product, or have a person give a live testimonial about how much they love being a distributor, you will keep the interest of new people who are listening for the first time.

For most of us, the first time in our lives we were ever presented with the concept of a live audience is back in Kindergarten when we played "Show and Tell." Everyone was always interested in what you were saying, because you were simply telling a story. We have all heard of the famous K.I.S.S. rule: Keep It Simple Stupid.

When presenting your business or product, the key play is to tell a story and keep it simple. Everyone can relate to the grandmother who can talk about their grandchild as the most beautiful, precious child in the world. She will make you feel as if her grandchild would be such a gift to have. You need to take that same simplicity and utilize it during your presentation and create the same result - ownership of your product.

As you tell stories, people will remember those stories versus all the facts in the world. Facts tell, but stories sell. They will get involved in your business and/or purchase your product, because of all of the success stories that you told. People will love to be part of a winning team. Storytelling keeps people tied in to you and your presentation. When in doubt during a presentation, tell a story in order to bring people's attention back to you.

When I present, I ALWAYS tell many stories because when I was first introduced to direct sales what perked my ears was a story of a young lady who had a lifestyle I wanted. The personal story of her lifestyle is what made me decide to get involved in the business. In that business, I went on to build an enormous organization, and all that I did was tell my story and the company's story over and over!

Combine the key strategy of storytelling along with the correct mindset, and you will achieve your wildest dreams through your Network Marketing business!

Fundamental #7 - The Power of the A to Z Presentation

Over the last 20+ years of being an international motivational speaker, capitalism marketing strategist and business coach. I've been asked on a regular basis, *"John, what is the #1 reason why people fail in their own Network Marketing Business?"*

What do I say to them? I say with 110% confidence that it's because they customize their presentations to each person and assume what their prospect will find exciting. This mindset will definitely set you up for failure!

The key to success is the power of duplication, showing the exact same presentation over and over. You need to be presenting the entire business from A-Z to each and every one of your prospects, because you have no idea what is going on inside them as you share the business. During my Boot Camps, I teach about the concept of daily, laser-focused consistent duplication.

Simply, the #1 ingredient in your MLM success equation is a duplicable presentation. You need to show your business exactly the same each time you present for two primary reasons:

Reason #1 - You will be 100% full of confidence & conviction knowing what you are going to say, because you have presented the entire plan from A-Z numerous times the SAME EXACT WAY. Repetition is the #1 skill of all MLM millionaires.

Reason #2 - I can almost guarantee that when you begin to put this into practice you will have your prospects respond to aspects of your business that you would have assumed they would not have been interested in before. You will see your business explode within a short period of time.

Just imagine everyone in your network internalizing this mindset and fully understanding the power of an A - Z presentation. The leadership abilities within them will skyrocket, which will in turn create momentum in your network marketing business.

Momentum is a force that you will not be able to control; it is also the key to unprecedented growth in your business. Leadership is earned by people who deserve it, and you will project leadership when you present with the power of A - Z. Always remember, it's just a matter of time before you hit your target when you keep aiming for it!

I have proven to be a true master of creating A-Z presentations. During my years in Network Marketing, I did it over and over again until I built an international team of over 25,000 representatives in 10 countries. Do you believe that you can do this too? Sure you can! Go for it Champion!

Fundamental #8 - That Little Bit Extra

The "little bit extra" is a very powerful concept to put into practice in every aspect of your life. The difference between being ordinary and being extraordinary is that little bit EXTRA. The little bit extra is what separates average performers from CHAMPIONS!

In the MLM recruiting process, the little bit extra is that one extra follow-up call, that extra sincere thank-you or the extra little bit of energy that you put into the presentation of your business. This will separate you from your competition!

You can either go through the motions of your business, or you can give that little bit extra in order to cement yourself in the mind of your potential team member. We all can relate to purchasing a product/service from someone who just gave a little bit extra attention than their competitor did and THAT is the reason we bought from THEM!

When I strategically coach someone, one major objective is to move that person to become a Champion in their field. One of the easiest ways is to show them the value of what a little extra eye contact with their prospects or customers brings. You need to look your prospect or customer directly in their eyes when you are presenting your business.

This drives your confidence and conviction into them, and they begin to realize what you and your product/service have to offer them. When I coach people, I tell them that the eye contact strategy alone will take them two major steps ahead of their competition.

Remember, people will feed off your confidence from the look in your eyes. As you progress in your journey towards fulfilling your WHY, you need to constantly give that little extra! The true sign of a Champion-to-be is just when it seems impossible for him/her to give that extra push they dig deep down and give that little bit extra to fulfill their WHY!

During my events, I teach the attendees about having the mindset of always giving a little bit more than their competitor. Over the long run, it will pay off big! A small improvement over a long period of time will produce outstanding results in your MLM business and catapult you towards the achievement of your Why in life.

Now that you know the benefit of giving that little bit of extra focused effort, you need to ask yourself a question, "What can I do today and every day with a little more effort to move me to the Champion level in my MLM business?" You must realize someone will be the Champion in your MLM company. Why not you? I believe that YOU are the one!

Bonus Report

The Top *10* Million Dollar
Recruiting Tips
to Explode your MLM Business
NOW

Recruiting Tip #1: Recruit up - stop talking to people who can simply fog up a mirror!

Take a look in the mirror and rate yourself on a scale from 1 to 10 based on your mastermind team, success in Network Marketing, habits, etc. Now, let's say that you are a "7".   From that point on, you must decide to only recruit people that you consider to be a "7" or higher.

Why? Because it is easy to recruit down or in other words to recruit people that you feel you have control over. You must make a decision right now to recruit Champions...

People with self-confidence, a high level of personal belief, a positive attitude and you'll build a multi-million dollar MLM team.

**Recruiting Tip #2: Always have a
Contact Card with you not a business
card. This will earn you financial
freedom in MLM.**

You do not need a business card with a
lengthy website, email address or several
phone numbers. This makes it impossible for
anyone to get in touch with you especially
prospects because of simple confusion

Instead, only have basic contact information
that allows people to easily call you and
schedule a time for you to share your MLM
business opportunity with them.

A "contact card" should contain your name,
phone number and title – International
Champion Recruiter. No more, No less.

Yes, you are an International Champion
Recruiter so give out a card that gives
everyone that impression and changes their
lives forever.

Recruiting Tip #3: Make recruiting a daily habit by role-playing with your team and become a recruiting machine.

You must realize that you are a Recruiting Machine not a Product Pusher. You don't have to be an expert on your product line, company history or even the Network Marketing industry. Allow your company to do those things for you.

You are a Recruiter, and you must make recruiting a daily habit. Practice your recruiting style with your MLM team. Yes, every single day! Remember, your habits will predict your future.

Recruiting Tip #4: Contacting three people per day must be your daily goal in order to build a Million Dollar MLM Business.

Networkers such as yourself get "Fired Up" after a conference call, seminar or boot camp, then go home and call 25 people in which you are likely rejected by 24 of those people. What happens? You are automatically filled with self-doubt along with fear and simply refuse to make any more calls.

Commit to contacting only '3' people per day, and your business will explode. Yes only three....This commitment along with the other tips that you have learned in this book will build your belief and shape you into a Network Marketing Millionaire Champion Extraordinaire and live absolute Lifestyle Freedom.

Recruiting Tip #5: Instead of you needing people to make your MLM business successful, develop the mindset that people need what you have in your business to become successful in life.

The only person that you "need" to be a successful MLM recruiter is YOU!

Your belief in your business must be strong, and you must truly believe that your business will ultimately make others successful too!

The success of your business isn't based on your ability to recruit that one certain person. Your belief, habits, mindset and heart will enable you to BUILD a Million Dollar M.L.M. Business. Once again...The only person that you "need" in your business to be a successful recruiter is YOU!

Your belief in yourself and your business must be evident to your prospect so that they truly understand that your business vehicle will assist them in achieving lifestyle freedom.

Recruiting Tip #6: Your commission check is determined by the number of people that you recruit.

That's right...your commission check is not based on your knowledge of the products, your history of the company, etc. The amount of people that you recruit who become leaders will directly control you becoming a Network Marketing Millionaire!

Yes, you read this right! Your check solely depends on the amount of quality recruits you develop into long-term focused leaders or your team

So, stop wasting your time memorizing the product ingredients, company perks, etc.

Decide today to become a Recruiting Machine in order to develop a highly profitable, life-changing MLM Millionaire Team!

Recruiting Tip #7: Recruiting is and will always be the foundation of your financial freedom.

The "foundation" is the most important part of any large, powerful structure. If there are any cracks in the foundation of a skyscraper, then it will crumble.

Recruiting is the foundation of your Networking Marketing business and must be solid in order for you to become financially free. Build a strong foundation by immersing yourself in personal development material, attending team building events plus Events that we Host

I believe 100% in hammering this point home! Don't fool yourself into thinking that you can become a recruiting machine when your entire life and business are set upon a shaky foundation. It will eventually crumble, and nothing will ever change for you.

Recruiting Tip #8: The art of active listening is the key to effectively recruiting MLM Champions.

So many networkers "talk" their prospects completely out of sponsoring into their business by rambling on. It's like diarrhea of the mouth!

When you learn to be an effective listener and master the art of active listening, you will be able to understand your prospect and how your business opportunity will dramatically impact their lives.

The key is to understand your prospect. You see their reason for deciding to join your team maybe different than yours. When you develop the fine art of active listening, you'll see your MLM team explode!

Recruiting Tip #9: Follow-up with your Champion prospect within 24 to 48 Hours of your initial A-Z presentation.

Many champion prospects and several thousands of dollars have passed right through your hands, because you haven't kept the momentum flowing after your initial contact with your prospect.

You must follow-up within 24-48 hours not four or five days later after calling the prospect, giving him/her a contact card or inviting him/her to an A- Z Business Presentation. You must follow-up in a timely manner (24-48 hours) and continue to build that relationship between you and your soon to be Champion Teammate.

This follow-up recruiting tip will keep the momentum flowing and make you a rock-solid, laser-focused, fired-up, hugely successful Champion recruiter!

Recruiting Tip #10: Every single day the next MLM Million Dollar Earner will walk right by you; therefore, you must make the decision to recruit them at that moment before someone else grabs a hold of the opportunity.

Don't be afraid to stick your hand out and introduce yourself or give a prospect your contact card. You will regret not prospecting that person when you see him/her at the next local business presentation after someone else took the step that you didn't.

As you look around to prospect, you never know who will be right for the business. Allow the individual to make the decision to build a dynasty after you show the A to Z presentation.

SPECIAL BONUS

Since you invested your time in reading this material and you are serious about building your MLM business, I would like to offer you a very Special Bonus. Call or Text our Elite Team at (561) 847-3467 or Email Team@ConservativeBusinessJournal.com and say "I want my Special MLM Bonus Now!" You will absolutely love it. You are a Champion, and I believe in you 1,000%!